Skateboarding Welcomes You all

by Jovon Vest the Best

skate flick

youtube TRICK TIPS BEGINNER look up skate tricks from this book

safety first
helmets
elbow pad
knee pad
hand gaurd
long socks
skateboard shoes like
vans or ES

make sure your skateboard is ready to ride

by making sure everything tighten down
grip bolts popping up are they smooth
wheels chips gum
bearings missing or crack
hardwire tight and no broken bolts
trucks tight till where it's not going to
fall off broken board chips cracks nuts
loose wheel nuts to tight wheels don't spend
trucks lose or tight for turning
wheels soft or tight
the size boards min. 7.25.7.5. 7.75 8.
8.25. 838. 8.5. 875. 9.
phillip bolts or alii keys

Types of Skateboarding
street skating: skating on streets, curbs, benches, handrails and other elements of urban and suburban landscapes.
vert skating: skating on ramps and other vertical structures specifically designed for skating.
half pipe: a U-shaped ramp of any size, usually with a flat section in the middle

vert ramp: a half-pipe, usually at least 8 feet tall, with steep sides that are perfectly vertical near the top.

parts of the skateboard

1.deck:
2.grip tape:
nose:Top of board
tail: bottom
the trucks connect to the deck
3.trucks: hold the wheels
4.wheels: hond the bearings
5.bearing makes you roll
6.hardwire
maybe risers

how to take care of a skateboard

keep away from water
grip gum is used for grip tape for extra
fresh grip
you can sand the side of the board
wth griptape to make it feel fresh
spray paint makes your board slippery
bs means backside
fs mean frontside in front of you
take turns but keep trying

watch out for
other skaters
animals
cars and busses
bikes people kids
rocks
tree branch
seeds from trees
bees
cracks
water
nails in ramps
holes in ramps
unsafe ramps
unsafe rails
bearings broken
trucks broken
hardwire broken

in the grass make the board go up and down make the board turn
jump off the board dont skate if it's windy

typesof ollies

ollie fakie

Ollie North

Ollie South

ollie west

nollie

switch ollie

sexchange

ollie feet twist

Chinese Ollie

Drop-In Manuals Tic-Tac

always be respectful
if someone is hurt ask are you ok
because if your hurt they should ask
you if your ok
don't get upset keep trying or try a
different trick
100 tricks to perfect
skateboarding in the streets driving the
car will never be the same see that
spot
watch out for everything bombing hills

left handed
right handed
left foot first
or left foot first

pushing and stopping

brab walk

rollin

power slde

hippy jump

cave man

primo

bomb drop

Body Varial

foot placements and knees bent

Basic Tricks

bs 180
fs 180
pop shuvit
fakie ollie

healing scars and marks use
sha butter everyday

roll in roll out 24 hours skateboarding you cant stop that. sorry i just made you a rapper.i need to teach you how to be a skateboarder a good one at that

No Comply

boneless

boneless 180

old school

kflip

boneless flip

shuvit
360 shuvit
540 shuvit
shuvit vs pop shuvit

skaters should have aways

skate kit
shoes
underward
jeans
socks
deck
wheels
water
snacks
bearings
maybe trucks
hardwire
money for the bus or taxi

meeting ppl and how skating will change
your life
say hi to other skaters say you skate too
most ask whats your best trick i might say
nollie full cab or bigger flip
jump on board
turning the board in your hand
two board manny
nose grab pop shuvit
keep spinning till your spins are smooth
learn how to bail on flat rail and ramps
running up the ramp
blunt using hand
bam drop in
5050 fackie
nosestall 180 out
2 rock and roll
old school 180
shoot board from feet
old school shovit

skateboarding is one big family all
over the world
i've been skating for over 22years
learn from   a professional
i was one of three stars from
camp woodward season 3 on fuel.tv

switch

riding the other way

Manual
Nose Manual
One Foot Manual
One Wheel Manual

riding on one or two wheels only can
be used as a combo

mimi ramp

the feeling of the ramp up and down
kickturn
pumping
bs axle stall
bs axle grind
bs 5.0 stall
fs axle stall
fs axle grind
fs 5.0 stall
fs smith
back smith
blunt stall
krook stall
krook stall hurricane stall
feeble stall
nose stall
tail stall
pivot stall

rock to fakie

Bs rock and roll

Fs rock and roll

switch fs rock and roll

switch bs rock and roll

fakie bs rock fakie

fakie fs rock fakie

fakie fs rock and roll

fake bs rock and roll

fakie axle

fakie smith

fakie feeble

bs and fs disaster

switch blunt

noseblunt

nose pick

sugercane

flip rocc
flip rocc and fs roll
flip rock bs out
heel rock fakie
heel rock n roll
heel rock bs out
360 flip rock
vheel rock
vflip rock
360 rock
rock sex change
fackie tail

mini ramp combos

bs feeble stall 270 out
fs feeble stall 270 out
blunt 5.0
blunt rock
bunt rock and roll
blunt feeble 270 out
blunt flip rocc
blunt flipout
oilly u bs 5050

spins turning

90 fs or bs

180

270

360

540

720

900

mctwist

fs big spin

bs big spin

fakie bs big spin

fakie fs big spin

nollie fs big spin

nollie bs bigspin

slides

bluntslide

boardslide

nose

tail

lipslide

darkslide

grinds

50-50 Grind
Backside 5-0
Backside 50-50
feeble
crook
over crook
nose
tail
salad
smth
suski
barly
whillie
layback
primo
hurricane
sugercane
slash

nollie

rolling with feet up front opposite of ollie

fackie

rolling backwards fakie

rails

grinds and slides are done on rails also
you can skate over the rail

stairs

doing tricks down stairs and up

banks

you go up and down or into.
bank over bar

curbs

are everywhere skaters wax this up for
slides and grinds
also there are many ways into a curb

late flips
spins and bigger

grabs

benihana
double grab
indy grab
tuck knee
tail grab
nose grab
melon
stalefish
roast beef grab

airs

air walk

backflip

chrst air

fs air

bs air

japan air

muteair

judo air

acid drop

bomb drop

hippy jump
firecrcker
primo
pogo
sexchange flip and spins
wallriide
wallie
street plant
primo grind
no complay 180
dizzy jv made
bs power slide
bean plant
layback slide
egg plant
stablegun

the flip list can be used as a combo of reg fakie switch and nollie

Flips

kflip
hflip
vflip
vheel
360 flip
360 heel
hard flip 360
hard fliip
540 flip
720 flip
fs flip
bs flip
bs full cab flip
fs full cab flip
bs half cab flip
fs half cab flip
bs full cab heel
bs half cab heel
fs full cab heel
fs half cab heel
big flip

bs heel
fs heel
casper flip
360 with a hflip
360 witha kflip
big heel
bigger flip
bigger heel
alphaflip
inward heel
giger fliip
forward flip
gazelle flip
getto biird
late flip
pressure fliip
under flip

double and triple Flips

back foot flips and spins
late turns
shiftyflips

look up on
youtube tip tricks
if help need

impossibles

raps around your
foot

some of my tricks i custom made over the years

5050 fs nollie 180 5050
Fakie shove 5050 bs 180 out
180 switch 5050 fakie fs 180 5050
Board slide 5050 flip out
270 tail
Nollie flip bs tail
Nollie flip crook
Nollie heel 5050
Switch tail both ways
Switch crooks both ways
Fakie flip grind
Nollie flip fs tail
Nollie shove 5050 360 nollie shove out
Nollie shove fs nollie 180 out

Fakie flip bs 5050
Fakie flip noseslide
Willie grind nollie 360 both willies
Willie 180 out both ways
Fakie switch crook 180 out
Fakie 180 bs nose grind bs 180 out
5050 360 flip out or 360
Switch 180 febal
Nollie nose bunt
Fakie blunt
Nollie bs smith 180 out
Switch board 180 5050
Switch 5050 bs 180 5050
Half cab flip board
Wille 5.0
nollie flip 5050 both ways
nollie heel 5.0

Bs board switch 5050 180 out
Switch board 5050
Switch board 180 board
Switch board nose grind
Bs 180 fakie smith
Fakie Big spin blunt
5050 nollie shove out both ways
Nollie smith shove out
Fs 5050 bs switch feeble fs 180 out
Fakie cab crook bs 180 out
180 switch sukee

skate facts

crazy combos

crook flip out
crook heel out
flip krook
kflip lipslide
360 out of anything
flip out anything
heel out anything

fresh gear

new shoes

new board

new wheels

you land better feel
better

skating cost
boards $20-120
shoes $20-150 every week or month
wheel $10-40 last long
Trucks $40-60 a pair last long
bearings $5-150
grip $5-10
long socks $10
skateparks some free some cost
hardwire $3-10

skateboard opportunity

skate contest sponsorships
riding for a skate team tours
meeting new people
role model
prize
free support
youtube
tv shows and movies
newspaper
skate for a event Skateboard industry jobs range from working as a professional skater, performing videography or photography at events, working in advertising or merchandising, becoming a reporter or journalist, working in design with skateboards, skateparks, or merchandise, or working at or managing a skatepark.

skate brands not ever skate brand supports
skating most brands are only in skating for the
money

Element
MOB GRIP
Airwalk
Plan B Skateboards
·187 Killer
5Boro Skateboards
Brooklyn Projects
Krooked Skateboards
Happy HourHappy Socks
Enjoi
Tensor Trucks
Penny Skateboards
Triple 8
Santa Cruz Skateboards.
Founded: 1973. ...
·Powell Peralta. Founded: 1976. ...
·Girl Skateboards. Founded: 1993. ...
·Anti-Hero Skateboards. Founded: 1995. ...
·Enjoi. Founded: 2000. ...
·Baker Skateboards. Founded: 2000. ...
·Real Skateboards. Founded: 1991. ...
·Polar Skate Co. Founded: 2011.

Emerica
Lakai
DC Shoes
Vans
Adidas
Converse
Nike SB
Ace
Anti Hero
Almost
Baker
DGK

we skate for fun we skate for the
people that cant
we skate for charities
we skate for the skate friends that
passed
skateboarding is not a crime

BOWL & POOL GAP MANUAL PAD FUNBOX & PYRAMIDE POLE
Skateboarding was first invented in the 1950s in California. The skateboard's origin began in California and Hawaii, The 1930s was the beginning of skateboarding, and surfing sidewalk surfingWomen, of course, are not new to the sport of skateboarding—since the skateboard was invented in California sometime around the middle of the 20th century, women such as Patti McGee, Peggy Oki, Kim Cespedes, and Laura Thornhill The first significant skateboarding boom was in 1963, and then popularity waned over the years until 1972 when urethane wheels were introduced That means that 2.9% of US citizens stepped on a skateboard at some time that year. That's useful. 6.3-million skateboarders in the United States The early wheels on skateboards were made of clay or metal. Polyurethane wheels were not invented until the early 1970s. Skateboards are made with seven layers of maple plywood.

Skateboarding is considered to be one of the world's top 10 sports today.

Despite its popularity there are less than 500 skateboard parks in the United States. To raise money for these parks, professional skateboarders took part in golfing tournaments. The first professional female skateboarder was Patti McGee. Women have been involved in the sport since it was first created. atti McGee is a former professional skateboarder. She was the 1964 Women's first National Skateboard Champion, Santa Monica. Her first skateboard was built by her brother in wood shop from her own shoe skate as a surprise. Her second skateboard was a
The most famous skateboard trick is the "ollie", created by Alan Ollie Gelfand in 1978.

security
run run
some skate spots
people don't want
anyone to skate
there or over there

skate histoy

Skateboarding was banned in Norway between 1978 and 1989 due to the number of injuries to skateboarderIt is estimated that over 800,000 skateboarders visit the doctor in the United States each year because of skateboarding injuries. One of the world's most famous skateboarders is Tony Hawk. He owns Birdhouse - a skateboarding company More than 18 million people in the United States own a skateboard. Roughly 74% are males and 85% are under the age of 18 Skateboarding has many benefits for participants, including increasing concentration, improving hand-eye coordination. Skateboarding improves the skateboarder's metabolism, improves their balance, provides creative freedom, and increases their fitness levelOne

levelOne of the first methods to jump while riding a skateboard was called "Gorilla Grip" and involved wrapping one's toes around the board and jumping Before its introduction, skateboard wheels were often made of metal or clay. With the introduction of polyurethane wheels came a massive surge of interest and the birth of street skateboarding There are two stances when riding a skateboard Hawaiian Holiday" featuring Mickey & Minnie Mouse, Pluto, Donald Duck, and you guessed it, Goofy who is shown riding right-foot forward. Both goofy and regular footed are considered "natural stances Most professional skateboarders are ambidextrous The first parks designed specifically for skateboarding appeared in the early 1970's Skateboarding tricks are broken down into several categories.

The world record for the longest unassisted flatground ollie goes to professional skateboarder Jordan Hoffart at 16 feet, 6 inches. Skate stoppers
No pain, no gain
skateboarding finally becomes an Olympic sport
Skateboarding is the sixth most popular sport in the world
warren Bolster was one of the first to use fish-eye lenses for skateboard photography

1940s–1960s
surfing on the sidewalk 1970s, Frank
Nasworthy started to develop a
skateboard wheel made of
polyurethane,
Go Skateboarding Day june 21
skate video games are fun

skate videos

Powell Peralta

The Bones Brigade Video Show

H-Street

Blind

Alien Workshop

Plan B

Girl Skateboards

World Industries

Shorty's

Zero

Emerica

Baker 2G

Flip

Fully Flared

some legend skaters
Jovon Vest

tony hawk won the most
vert competitions.

plg
mike mo
chaz ortiz
andy macdonald
figgy
brian herman
mike vailly
kevin romar

Theotis Beasley

Corey Duffel

Jagger Eaton

Erik Ellington

Tom Penny

Manny Santiago

Bastien Salabanzi

Mark Suciu

John Cardiel

Mike Carroll

Leo Romero

Wes Kremer

Tony Alva
Christian Hosoi

Rodney Mullen made almost every trick

Rob Dyrdek
Ryan Sheckler
Bob Burnquist
Steve Caballero
Paul Rodriguez Jr.
Bam Margera
Danny Way
Chris Cole
Andrew Reynolds
Mark Gonzales
Mike Carroll
Lance Mountain
Jamie Thomas
Mark Appleyard
Chico Brenes

Rip great people

shaine cross

zane timson

Harold Hunter

Pepe Martinez

Lewis Marnell

Dylan Rieder

jake Phelps

Jay J. Adams rip

Made in the USA
Las Vegas, NV
14 September 2023

77565736R00046